The Shore Flies

Gabriele
Publishing House

The Shore Flies
Liobani School Sophia

From the book: *Liobani: I Advise—Do You Accept?*

1st Edition, March 2024
© Gabriele-Verlag Das Wort GmbH
Max-Braun-Str. 2, 97828 Marktheidenfeld
www.gabriele-verlag.com
www.gabriele-publishing-house.com

Translated from the original German title:
"Die Sumpffliegen
Liobani-Schule Sophia"

The German edition is the work of reference
For all questions regarding the meaning of the contents.

All rights reserved
Order No. S619EN
Printed by: KlarDruck GmbH, Marktheidenfeld, Germany
ISBN: 978-3-96446-528-3

Liobani-Schule Sophia
for young and old

Dear friends, surely you are asking what one can learn in the Liobani School and who Liobani is.
Liobani is an angel being from heaven, a daughter of the ray of Wisdom and gives us young and older human children, an understanding of the highest wisdom of heaven in simple words.

Liobani tells us about the path of our soul, about nature beings and about the rich life of nature, which is also our life.

In this way, she helps us to become a just and sincere person, and teaches us to treat all people, animals, plants, stones and everything that lives just as we ourselves want to be treated—because God, the Creator, is the life in all things.

Gabriele-Verlag Das Wort

The Shore Flies

Elf "Faith Little" reports

The elf Faith Little tells of her service, and how she was able to show the way again to someone who lost their way in the forest, and how the helping impulses she emitted flowed into the person's memory.

The person suddenly remembered where they came from and then knew to where they had to direct their steps to come out of the forest and find their way again.

Dear child,
you should know that
just as the guardian
angels know how to lead
people via their world of
sensations and senses,
so do the elemental
beings know how
to affect people's world
of sensations and senses,
without influencing
their free will.

The elf reports.
"Lost in thought, the man took one time this path and then another path in the woods, without paying attention to the trail signs that people put up for orientation. Thus, the man even left the path and went straight through the woods and through a thicket. Just as his thoughts had strayed, so did he also stray and lose his way.

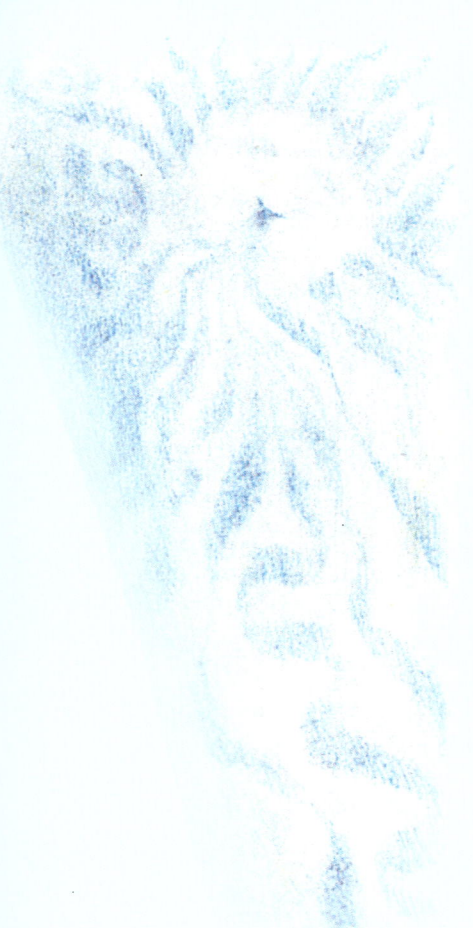

He saw neither the woods nor the thicket, and didn't even notice that he had left the path. He walked and walked and walked.

The elf Faith Little continued, "I tried to have an effect on him with my sensations, so as to help him. But this was not possible for me alone. And so, I called an air spirit and a fire spirit for help.

But even they couldn't get through to the hiker. The man became more and more immersed in his world of thoughts and in his fate. We elemental spirits had to let him keep on walking. But we stayed at his side; we accompanied him. At the same time, as impulses of awakening and help, we sent sensations of love. The hiker got tired and lay down on the woods' floor and fell fast asleep.

Now, a new possibility to help was given to me. I called the shore flies and instructed them about their task."

With their soft humming and with the beating of their wings, it is possible for them to calm a person's restless aura and to magnetize certain energy-poor areas of the body—or also to relax tense spots, so-called energy knots.

When the flies move in the aura of a sleeping person, they activate this magnetic field.

If the flies land on the body of the person, and then tickle these places, then the flies, the nature helpers, are trying to relax the tense nerves.

It is usually very annoying to a person, because it tickles and makes them nervous. But in reality, such flies are trying to help the person!

Y ou know, dear child, that like always attracts like. When certain types of flies are foreseen for these and similar purposes, that is, to magnetize and relax the human energy field, the aura, and the atmosphere, then this is their task for human beings, animals and nature, and they take their task seriously.

In most cases, however, this is irritating for the person, because they feel disturbed by the flies. Actually, the person's nervous system is disturbed, that is, tense, and the aura is also restless. That means that the magnetic field, the person's aura, is in disharmony.

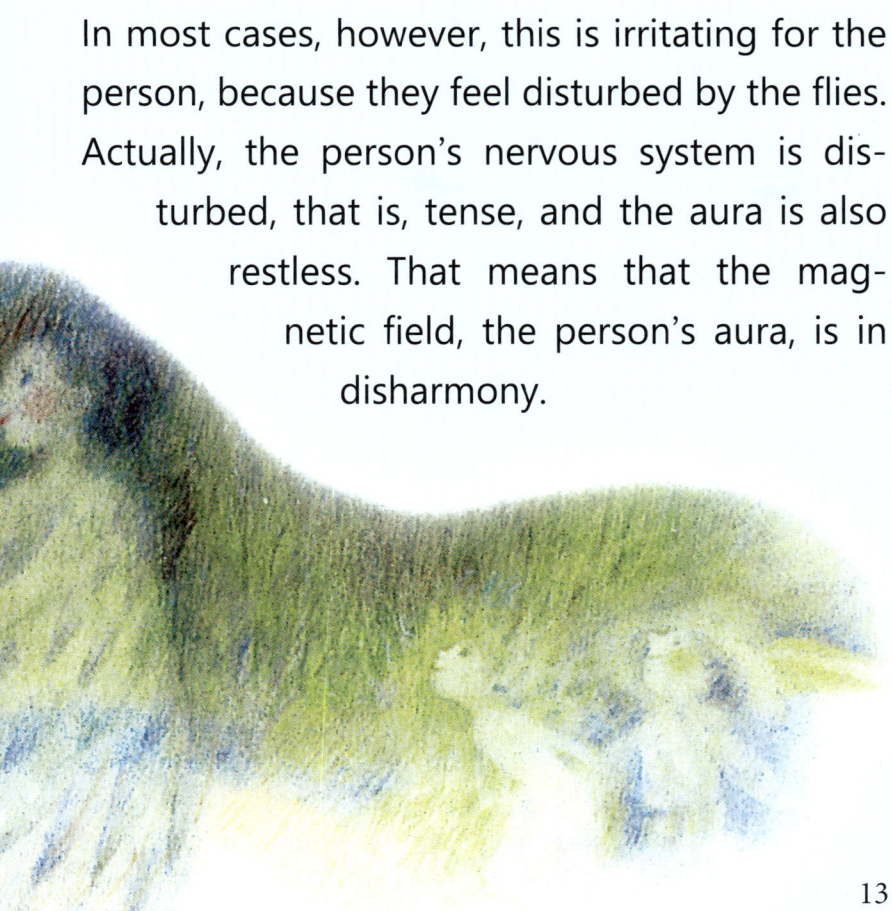

Thus, the flies buzz around sleepers and penetrate ever deeper into their aura, into their magnetic surroundings, until they have reached the body. They light on those places that are very tense.

The unpleasant irritation made by the flies makes the person do movements that normally would not be made, for example: The person hits out at the flies, slaps the arm, to drive the flies away or kill them.

But the flies purposely trigger this reaction in the person, so that—in our case—the hiker or sleeper touches his tense body part more strongly.

The result is that possible tensions or cramps there loosen up; the blood circulation increases, thus causing the brain cells to be supplied better with blood, so that now, by way of the person's world of sensations, the impulses of help from the nature beings reach the person's world of thoughts.

When you hear about shore flies, these are certain kinds of flies that don't bite. They have the task of bringing relaxation into the atmosphere, into nature, into people and animals, that is, to relieve tension.

And so, the flies' activity can also bring about a real relaxation in a person, so that the person is again receptive to positive, hopeful thoughts.

"So, the shore flies began their work," reported the elf.

"It took a long time until our hiker, who had fallen asleep, woke up again and finally got up. Before he woke up, he kept slapping himself more or less hard on his arm or foot, scratched his head or shook his whole body, to drive away the bothersome flies.

Now, he was totally awake, and looked around thinking: 'Where am I?'

I perceived this question to himself and made contact again. By way of his memory, that is, his world of sensations and senses, I showed him how he could find his way out of his bewilderment and recognize the way home.

So, via his memory world I stimulated his sense of sight and, at the same time, awoke further memories that gave him the assurance that he was reacting correctly, as he found his way out of the confusion of his human ego, in order to reach the path that led him homeward.

I was very happy when the hiker got up, stretched himself, looked at his watch, shook his head and said to himself: 'Well, it's high time I went home. I really slept deeply!'

He also thought: 'It was certainly good for me, because now, I see things more clearly. I now know the solution to the problem that upset me so much.'

He looked around and again said to himself: 'Ah, here's a path. I'll look for a trail sign and then I'll find my way out!'"

"Dear brothers and sisters," the elf then said to all the listening nature beings, "you can well imagine how very much the shore flies and I rejoiced that we could help!

The shore flies and I accompanied him for part of the way, and then we suddenly saw his guardian angel, who waved lovingly to us. We now knew: The hiker is in good hands."

Dear human brothers and sisters, you should know that if people are very upset and harbor dark, brooding thoughts and nurture them by pitying themselves, then the guardian spirit has to keep a greater distance from their charge because the person's aura is very restless and sparks of anger or hatred are being sent out.

The possibility of help, however, is manifold. Nature beings, air, fire and water spirits and many other positive forces are helpers for the material forms, for people, animals, plants and minerals.

When the elf had finished her report, the elder of the large family, "Mr. Rootman," a wise, that is,

already more matured, forest spirit, spoke great praise to the little, delicate elf. He asked her to invite the industrious shore flies for the next evening, when that part of the Earth turns away from the sun and the forest and meadow spirits carry out their sun dance, a prayer of thanks to the All-Spirit.

The elf was glad and sent out the invitation right away via waves of sensations. The shore flies answered via waves of sensations and gave thanks for the invitation, which, of course, they gladly accepted.

*Look—
There's more to read
and to listen to…*

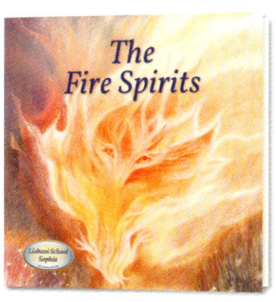

The Fire Spirits

Liobani talks about the nature helpers: the forces of fire, of the air, the water and of the earth. They work together with the nature spirit for the life in nature.

In this booklet you read about the fire spirits. What do they look like? What tasks do they have, and how do they work together with human beings?

From the book, "Liobani: I Advise—Do You Accept?".

Booklet, 28 pp., illustrated. 14 x 14 cm. ISBN: 978-3-96446-524-5

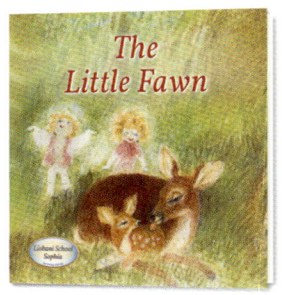

The Little Fawn

Elves and gnomes also are nature helpers.
The story of "The Little Fawn" shows us how the little elf "Go-with-Me" and the gnome "Hannilove" saved the little fawn that had broken a leg as it fled out of fear from a shot. Through this, we learn how the air spirit, the fire spirit and the kindness of a person helped in this rescue action.

From the book: "Liobani: I Advise—Do You Accept?"

Booklet, 40 pp., illustrated. 14 x 14 cm. ISBN: 978-3-96446-526-9

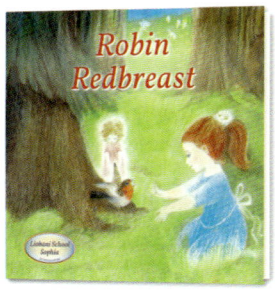

Robin Redbreast

The little robin became so frightened, that it could no longer fly—it feels pain and is calling for its mother.

What can be done?

Who can help it?

A story by Liobani from the life of animals, of elves and dwarfs, the invisible helpers of nature.

From the book: "Liobani: I Advise—Do You Accept?"

Booklet, 24 pp., illustrated. 14 x 14 cm. ISBN: 978-3-96446-525-2

Sly Fox

There are also nature beings responsible for the life of animals, plants and stones in the villages, towns and even cities. So read about how a being from the forest tells the story about the adventures of a fox, who dared to go too far away from his preserve and ended up being locked into the barn of a farm. And about the unique rescue action that took place!

From the book, "Liobani: I Advise—Do You Accept?".

Booklet, 30 pp., illustrated. 14 x 14 cm. ISBN: 978-3-96446-527-6

Dear children, dear parents and friends,
we will be happy to send you our current catalog
as well as free excerpts to many topics.

Gabriele Publishing House – The Word
Germany: Max-Braun-Str. 2, 97828 Marktheidenfeld, Germany

USA: P.O. Box 2221, Deering, NH 03244, USA

Toll-Free Order No.: +1-844-576-0937
International No.: +49(0)9391-504-843
www.gabriele-publishing-house.com